Gas
Attack!

e Canadians at

s, 1915

ory Series

CEF
1998

"Access to History; The Canadian History series:
Number 1"
Gas Attack! The Canadians at Ypres, 1915.
ISBN 1-896979-06-8

Published by: CEF BOOKS
                  P.O. 29123
                  3500 Fallowfield Road
                  Nepean, Ontario, K2J 4A9.

Editor-in-Chief: R.B. McClean

Access to History; The Canadian History Series

Number 2   Futility & Sacrifice: The Canadians on the Somme, 1916

Number 3   Winning the Ridge: The Canadians at Vimy, 1917

Number 4   Slaughter in the Mud: The Canadians at Passchendaele, 1917

Acknowledgements:
We would like to thank the Royal Canadian Legion Ontario Command branches for the support that made this book possible.

This book is dedicated to the memory of the Canadians who willingly gave their lives in the defence of freedom in the Twentieth Century. Lest We Forget.

Maps by Constable Enterprises, Stittsville, Ontario.
Graphics and Layout by Imágenes Graphic Arts, Ottawa, Ontario.

Front cover: "Canadians at Ypres" by W.B.Woolen, R.I.
(Courtesy Canadian War Museum, 91553)

Printed in Canada

Thursday, April 22, 1915 was a beautiful spring day in Belgium. The thousands of Canadian volunteer soldiers who had rushed to join the 'Colours' had easily weathered their first month of a so-far uneventful war in Europe. By the end of the weekend 2,000 of them would be dead after facing suffocating, poison gas and a numerically superior enemy. Canada would have paid its first 'bill' for the cause of King and Empire in the First World War.

EUROPE 1914-1918

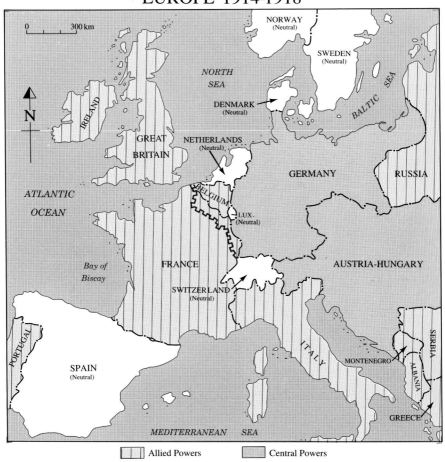

0   300 km

NORWAY
(Neutral)

SWEDEN
(Neutral)

NORTH
SEA

BALTIC SEA

DENMARK
(Neutral)

IRELAND

GREAT
BRITAIN

NETHERLANDS
(Neutral)

GERMANY

RUSSIA

BELGIUM

LUX.
(Neutral)

ATLANTIC
OCEAN

N

Bay of
Biscay

FRANCE

AUSTRIA-HUNGARY

SWITZERLAND
(Neutral)

PORTUGAL

SPAIN
(Neutral)

ITALY

MONTENEGRO

SERBIA

ALBANIA

GREECE

MEDITERRANEAN   SEA

Allied Powers   Central Powers

TABLE OF CONTENTS

Introduction vii

The Components of the 1st Canadian
Infantry Division at Ypres, 1915 ix

The Men Who Served 1

Overseas 5

To France and Flanders 5

The Battle Begins: Thursday, April 22, 1915 .9

Kitchener's Wood: Midnight, April 22/23, 1915 15

Mauser Ridge: Friday, April 23, 1915 17

The German Breakthrough: Saturday, April 24, 1915 20

After Shocks: Sunday, April 25, 1915 25

The Aftermath 27

Some Slang of the Great War 30

Technological Slaughter: The Use of Gas as a Weapon 31

In Flanders Fields 36

The Nationalities Who Served 37

Bibliography - Suggested Reading 38

GENERAL TRENCH-LINE ON THE WESTERN FRONT 1914-1918

Europe: 1914 - 1918

INTRODUCTION

When Great Britain declared war against Germany in August 1914, the Dominion of Canada was automatically at war. The young Dominion had just celebrated its 47th birthday; the provinces of Alberta and Saskatchewan had only joined Confederation nine years earlier. Canada was truly an infant nation. But it was proud of its part in the British Empire and many Canadians still considered themselves British first.

Like all the countries that declared war in 1914, Canadians reacted with enthusiasm. The thousands of men who flocked to the recruitment offices were eager to enlist and were anxious to reach the battlefields before the war was over. Most doubted the fighting would last until Christmas; few foresaw the four brutal years of attrition that lay ahead.

Prior to 1914, European wars had always been conducted to a set protocol; a couple of battles would be fought, negotiations would occur, a few colonies or some provinces would change hands and the war would be over. The First World War was different. It was to be total war and the belligerents were determined to fight to the finish.

The 19th Century had been a time of unprecedented technological innovation. Science and engineering had reached new heights and no where would their cruel application become more evident than on the battlefields of World War One. Artillery became more powerful and deadly, the machine gun, a still unknown weapon, would quickly win the support of Generals who had doubted its effectiveness, and the recently invented aeroplane would add a new dimension to the manner in which battles were fought. But, it was with the development of poison gases that a more insidious discovery was made. Killing by bullets and bombs was not new; killing by suffocating gases was.

It was at Ypres in April of 1915 that this terrible new weapon was first unleashed in force. With no known defence against poisonous gas, the unsuspecting Canadians, and the French Colonial troops beside them, were to experience the devastating effect of chlorine vapour. For the untried Canadians, the four days of the Second Battle of Ypres were to be a time of both triumph and tragedy.

THE MAKE-UP OF AN ARMY

The Army - The British Forces on the Western Front were divided into 4 or 5 Armies. The British Army in the field was commanded by Field Marshall Sir Douglas Haig. Throughout the war the British Army varied in strength, but usually employed 4,000,000 (1917) soldiers in the field. The Canadian Corps belonged to the 1st British Army, but had stints with the 4th Army as well.

The Army Corps - An Army Corps consisted of a number of Infantry Divisions, depending on its needs. The Corps was commanded by a Lieutenant-General. Its numeric strength varied, but could put as many as 120,000 men in the field. The Canadian Corps was made-up of 4 Divisions, all Canadian, but often had British Divisions attached for special attacks or battles.

The Division - The Infantry Division was composed of 3 Infantry Brigades and had 20,000 soldiers. It was commanded by a Major-General. The make-up of the 20,000 soldiers included 12,000 infantry, 3,500 artillerymen, 750 in a medical section, and 2,000 engineers and pioneers.

The Brigade - The Infantry Brigade was commanded by a Brigadier-General and consisted of 4 Battalions (4,000 infantrymen). Each Brigade had Engineers, signals, a field ambulance, trench mortar unit and machine gun unit.

The Battalion - The Infantry Battalion consisted of 1,000 men. This was the theoretical strength of the unit, after headquarters staff, illness, wounded, etc. were deducted, a Battalion would normally put 650 rifles into the line. It was commanded by a Lieutenant-Colonel. Each Battalion was made-up of 4 companies (200 men), commanded by a Major or Captain. In turn, the company was broken into 4 platoons commanded by a Lieutenant and each platoon into 4 sections commanded by a sergeant.

COMPONENTS OF THE 1ST CANADIAN INFANTRY DIVISION AT YPRES, 1915

1ST CANADIAN DIVISION

1ST INFANTRY BRIGADE	2ND INFANTRY BRIGADE	3RD INFANTRY BRIGADE
1ST BATTALION (WESTERN ONTARIO)	5TH BATTALION (SASKATCHEWAN)	13TH BATTALION (BLACK WATCH OF MONTREAL) REGIMENT)
2ND BATTALION (EASTERN ONTARIO)	7TH BATTALION (BRITISH COLUMBIA)	14TH BATTALION (ROYAL MONTREAL REGIMENT)
3RD BATTALION (TORONTO REGIMENT)	8TH BATTALION (90TH RIFLES OF WINNIPEG)	15TH BATTALION (48TH HIGHLANDERS OF TORONTO)
4TH BATTALION (CENTRAL ONTARIO)	10TH BATTALION (ALBERTA)	16TH BATTALION (CANADIAN SCOTTISH)

DIVISIONAL TROOPS:

1ST DIVISION CAVALRY: 19TH ALBERTA DRAGOONS
1ST CANADIAN DIVISION CYCLIST CORPS
1ST DIVISIONAL SIGNALS COMPANY
1, 2, AND 3 FIELD COMPANIES CANADIAN ENGINEERS
1, 2, AND 3 CANADIAN FIELD AMBULANCES

APPENDIX III.

WAR ESTABLISHMENT OF AN INFANTRY BATTALION FOR OVERSEAS SERVICE, 1915-16.

Headquarters.	C.E.F.	B.E.F.	Machine Gun Section.	C.E.F.	B.E.F.
Lieut-Colonel............	1	1	Subaltern................	1	1
Major....................	2	1	Sergeants	2	2
Adjutant.................	1	1	Corporals...............	1	1
Assistant Adjutant.....	1	0	Privates.................	24	24
Quarter-Master.........	1	1	Drivers, 1st line Tpt....	6	6
Signalling Officer.......	1	0	Batmen[2]................	1	1
Sergeant Major.........	1	1			
Quarter-Master Sergt..	1	1	Total......	35	35
Orderly Room Clerks[1].	1	2			
Sergeant Drummer....	1	0	Company.		
Sergeant Cook.........	1	1			
Transport Sergeant	1	1	Major (or Capt.)	1	1
Sergeant Shoemaker...	1	1	Capt. (2nd in Command)	1	1
Drivers, Transport.....	9	10	Subalterns...............	4	4
Drivers, spare animals.	2	2	Com. Sergt.-Major......	1	1
Batmen[2]	10	5	Com. Q.-M. Sergeant...	1	1
			Sergeants...............	8	8
Pioneers.			Drummers or Buglers..	4	0
			Corporals...............	10	10
Pioneer Sergeant......	1	1	Privates.................	188	192
Pioneers	10	10	Drivers, 1st line Tpt....	3	3
			Batmen[2]	6	6
Signallers.					
			Total......	227	227
Sergeant................	1	1			
Corporal................	1	1	Base Details.		
Privates[3]	15	15			
			Sergt. of the Band	1	0
			Sergeant Master Tailor	1	0
Stretcher Bearers......	16	16	Bandsmen..............	19	0
Orderlies for M.O.[4].....	2	2	Storemen[5]	4	0
			First reinforcement....	94	0
Total......	81	74			
			Total......	119	0
Attached.					
			Summary.		
Paymaster..............	1	0			
Medical Officer.........	1	1	Headquarters with		
R.A.M.C. for water duty			attached.............	89	82
Corporal	1	1	Machine Gun Section.	35	35
Privates..........	4	4	Companies[5] (4 of 227)....	908	908
Armourer	1	1	Base Details...........	119	
Interpreter..............	0	1			
Total......	89	82	Total......	1151	1025

[1] Orderly Room Clerk may be a sergeant or a corporal.

[2] Batmen are fully armed and trained soldiers and are available for duty in the ranks.

[3] Seven (7) may be lance corporals.

[4] One of the M.O.'s orderlies may be a sergeant (Medical Sergt.) and the other a lance corporal. The latter drives the cart for medical equipment.

[5] One storeman will mobilize with each company.

The Gas Attack at Ypres
April-May, 1915

THE MEN WHO SERVED

In 1914, Canada was a proud member of the most powerful Empire in the World. The majority of Canadians considered themselves British first, and being part of Great Britain's empire was a blessing. They willingly accepted the Mother Country's control over the fledgling Dominion's foreign policy, so when Great Britain declared war against Germany in August of that year, Canada was automatically at war. With a great sense of patriotism and to show support for the "Mother Country", Canada immediately offered Great Britain a contingent of 25,000 men. The offer was accepted and Canada began to mobilize for war.

Prior to 1914, Canada had a very small permanent army consisting of only 3,000 soldiers. Canada also had a large reserve force comprised of the many local militias. Being a member of a local militia regiment was not only patriotic, but was also socially desirable and always improved the profile of the man-about-town, whether he lived in Edmonton or Montreal. The militia units often carried impressive titles that were associated with famous British regiments. Militia names such as the Governor General's Foot Guards and the Duke of Connaught's Own Rifles emphasized Canada's close link to the British Crown. Many militia units reflected the country's Scottish heritage and to be a member of a kilted regiment like the Royal Highlanders of Canada was a source of immense pride. These were the men, officered by politicians and businessmen, who came together in 1914 to form the 1st Canadian Division.

A plan to mobilize Canada's armed forces for war had been arranged many years before, but the unpredictable Minister of Militia, Sam Hughes, scrapped the plans and substituted his own hastily devised scheme. Hughes ordered the militia units from across Canada to converge at an as-yet, unbuilt military camp at Valcartier near Quebec City.

Chaos ensued. May of the officers selected by Hughes to command the Valcartier camp were political cronies and possessed little talent for assembling and training an army. The change in mobilization plans also created jealousy among the militia units as officers, competing for the cherished overseas commands, eagerly attracted as many volunteers as possible into their units and then hurried them off to Valcartier. When the thousands of soldiers from across Canada began to pour into the unfinished camp, they were met with an operation in total disarray. Valcartier became hopelessly overcrowded. The training was disorganized. There were few capable instructors and there was insufficient equipment. Yet somehow during the following weeks the essence of a fighting force emerged and the 1st Canadian Division was born.

Slowly the recruits were weeded out and in the end more than 5,000 of the enthusiastic volunteers were discharged before the 1st Canadian Division left for the battlefields of Europe. Some 2,200 were declared medically unfit, 377 were released over the protestations of concerned wives and parents, and another 282 requested their own discharge. A further 610 were dismissed for misconduct, for refusing inoculation or for simply being 'insufficient'.

By mid-October, the Valcartier soldiers had received their basic training and had been assembled into battalions of approximately 1,000 men. Gone were illustrious militia titles like the Dufferin Rifles of Canada; in their place, each battalion was given a numbered identity.

One of these battalions, the 13th, was comprised of men from the former Royal Highlanders of Canada militia unit. Most of the men in the 13th Battalion were from Montreal and like all of the battalions, its officers were predominately well-to-do businessmen. Among the 13th's officers was Guy Drummond. The Drummond family was immensely rich and wielded great influence in the Canada of 1914. Guy, a handsome, 26 year-old banker, was already a millionaire. At 6' 3", he was a huge man for the times and towered above his men. Like so many of his contemporaries, he had been raised first to be a citizen of the British Empire and secondly to be a citizen of Canada. His intense loyalty to Great Britain, the Mother Country, dictated that the duty of every God-fearing Briton, including Colonials, was to defend the British Empire against the hated German Hun.

The 10th Battalion was made up primarily of soldiers from the disbanded Calgary Rifles militia. Their Commander was Russ Boyle. Boyle, a tough Alberta rancher, echoed Guy Drummond's resolve that the sun must never set on the British Empire. Like Drummond, Boyle was willing to sacrifice all, including his ranch and his family, to defend the Realm. However, he possessed few of Guy Drummond's polished, upper-crust mannerisms. The fact he was a lot rougher on the edges did not

Russell Boyle

Guy Melfort Drummond

detract from his effectiveness as an exceptional officer. On occasion, he used his ruggedness to discipline his men and once offered to fight one of his more difficult soldiers. The soldier declined to take up his offer.

The men who served under officers like Drummond and Boyle came from a wide variety of backgrounds. Many were labourers who worked on farms, in mines, on the railways, and in lumber camps. Others, often members of the middle class, lived in Canada's burgeoning cities and towns. They were men like Fred Fisher, a native of St. Catharines, Ontario, who joined Guy Drummond in the 13th Battalion. All were united in their determination to defend their Empire. As a group, they were moulded into the 1st Canadian Division - the men who would meet the gas at Ypres.

The men who formed the 1st Canadian Division were also remarkably diverse in other ways. The majority of the soldiers who assembled at Valcartier were recent immigrants who had come to Canada from the British Isles between 1880 and 1914. A breakdown reveals that only 30% (11% of these were French-Canadiens) were born in Canada and 64% were British immigrants. The remaining 6% were comprised of men who had emigrated from other countries, notably the United States and Russia. The officers, however, were predominately Canadian born. Clearly, these early volunteers had strong patriotic ties to the British Empire. Not surprisingly, Western Canada, which had been the destination of many of the recent immigrants, provided a disproportionate number of enlistees.

There were other reasons why these men volunteered to join the Canadian Expeditionary Force. The prospect for adventure, a change from the humdrum of daily life or just doing the 'right thing' were important motivations. A sizeable number had served in the Boer War and many had been raised on stories that glorified the British Empire. All of these factors contributed to their enthusiasm. Most believed the war would be over by Christmas; few anticipated the war would endure for so long and be so bloody.

In October 1914, the 30,000 men (including 101 Nursing Sisters) of the 1st Canadian Contingent sailed for Great Britain. As the long line of ships moved down the St. Lawrence River from Quebec City, none of their passengers could have foretold the terror of the gas they would face at Ypres. Whether they were members of the Queen's Own Rifles of Canada from Toronto or the Royal Highlanders of Canada from Montreal, these men were soon to face an experience from which few would emerge unscathed.

OVERSEAS

The 1st Canadian Contingent arrived in Plymouth, England in mid-October, 1914. They were moved to a tent-camp on the Salisbury Plain, in the south of England, near Stonehenge. The British had not been prepared for the arrival of so many Canadians, and just like at Valcartier, bad planning created chaos. Far worse than Valcartier was the horrible English winter that awaited them. Months of frigid drizzle continually tested the Canadians. The cold and damp weather froze the men in their tents and even the hardiest farmer from Saskatchewan must have felt the damp winter in England was the coldest he had ever encountered.

Just like Valcartier, they somehow muddled through. There was some training, a few rounds of target practice and lots of marching. All of which would be of little practical use once they finally reached the front and faced the Germans. In February 1915, the 1st Canadian Division received embarkation orders for France. After six months of preparation, they were finally going to come face-to-face with the Hun.

TO FRANCE AND FLANDERS

The 20,000 men of the 1st Canadian Division crossed the English Channel and disembarked at St. Nazaire on the French coast in February 1915. After several days of confusion, they were finally marched to a new camp where they waited for their equipment to arrive and did some light training. Their first taste of war came when they entered the trenches in a quiet sector, near Fleurbaix, on the French-Belgian border. At Fleurbaix, they were introduced to trench warfare, the mud, the rats, and the constant fear of sudden death by snipers, trench mortars or artillery. It was at Fleurbaix that the first Canadians died, mostly shot through the head by expert German snipers or killed by shrapnel released in the overhead explosions of artillery shells. By First World War standards, this trench 'wastage' was insignificant.

In April 1915, the 1st Canadian Division received orders to leave the Fleurbaix sector and move into the trench-line northeast of the ancient Belgian city of Ypres. It was at Ypres that the Germans had tried to crack the British line in the fall of 1914. Attacking in swarms, they were shot down by the rapid rifle fire of the British troops. The bodies of German, British and French soldiers killed in 1914 still lay where they had fallen,

5

rotting in the spring sun. The odour of decaying flesh, which became synonymous with the Ypres area, mixed with the sweet spring air.

The desperate fighting in 1914 had produced a bulge or salient in the British line west of Ypres that protruded into German-held territory. By April 1915, the Ypres 'salient' had become one of the most dangerous places on the entire Western Front. The bulge in the trench-line enabled the Germans to fire into the British positions from behind, from either the north or the south. This constant threat of a German attack from in front or from behind made the positions the Canadians occupied one of the most feared places to be in the line.

On a grander scale, the Ypres salient was vulnerable to a major German attack. At any time, the Germans, attacking from the north and south, could attempt to pinch-off any troops in the bulge. If they were successful in cutting off the British positions from behind, there would be no avenue of escape for the Canadians.

The Germans also had the advantage of topography on their side. The city of Ypres is located on the Flanders plain, an area distinguished by flat, low-lying terrain. Occasionally, the land rises to form insignificant ridges to a height of 40 to 60 metres. In the spring of 1915, control of these ridges was of great importance, for they offered the occupier the ability to observe all of the opponent's movements and to direct deadly artillery fire accurately onto the enemy's positions. All of the main ridges, running like a crescent around Ypres, were controlled by the Germans, with the exception of a few minor crests close to the city that were to be occupied by the Canadians.

"The right flank and the next portion to the left had a parapet of mud heaped up in front approximately 2 feet thick at the bottom and from 4 inches to 1 foot at the top with the occasional loophole punched through the earth...In front of these sections are numerous dead bodies in a decomposed state lying on the surface of the ground, also in the trench itself and round about there are numerous bodies buried at a very shallow depth making it impossible to excavate at all...There is also human excreta littered all over this place...This trench has no traverses and is directly enfiladed from the German trenches to the north."

Captain T.C. Irving, Canadian Engineers.

Another rude shock awaited the Canadians. As they entered their new lines, they were unsettled by what they found. If the thousands of decaying bodies bothered them, taking over the defences left by the departed French was far more disturbing and also very dangerous.

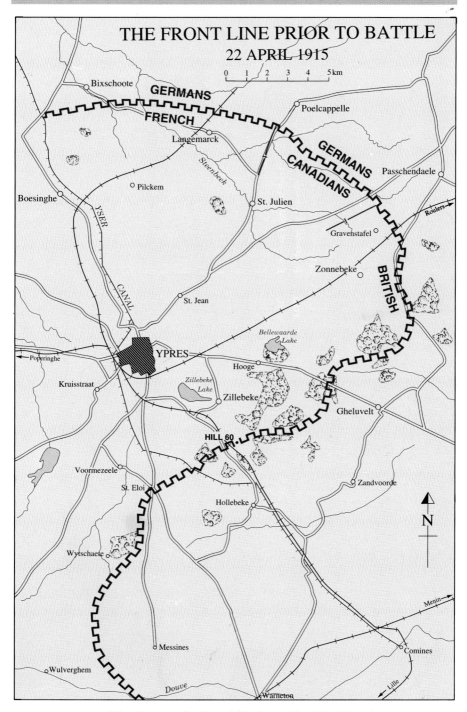

The Ypres Salient; Before the Battle

The French had made little effort to dig in and their front-line defences were not connected. Instead, they had relied on a series of half-moon positions, with limited protection from sandbags and almost no barbed wire out in front to impede an attack by German infantry. In many cases, the thin sandbag walls protecting the men were incapable of stopping the enemy's rifle bullets. Immediately, the Canadians began to strengthen and expand the weak defences they had inherited, but time was running out. It was now April 20, 1915.

Ominous intelligence reports indicating that the Germans were about to use a deadly new weapon had reached the Canadians. The weapon was poisonous gas. A German deserter had revealed how the enemy was bringing thousands of cylinders filled with gas into their trenches. When the wind was blowing in the right direction, the valves on the cylinders would be opened and a huge cloud of suffocating gas would float towards the Canadian lines. When the Canadians were all dead or incapacitated, the German infantry would attack and capture Ypres.

Unfortunately, the General Staff and other high-ranking officers did not take the vital information seriously enough. Even if they had, what could they do against a weapon for which they had no defence? The Canadians had no choice but to continue to strengthen their defences and to await whatever might befall them.

GENERAL INTELLIGENCE:
According to prisoners of the XV German Army Corps the ZILLEBEKE front is provided with iron bottles 5 feet high placed slightly behind the trenches, either buried or sheltered. These bottles contain asphyxiating gas. They have not yet been used but pioneers have been instructed in their use. They are laid prone and the seal removed, when the gas escapes parallel to the surface of the earth. A favourable wind is necessary. The pioneers in charge are provided with special apparatus fixed on their heads as a protection against the fumes. The inventor has been promoted to a lieutenant. (This is on the authority of the 111th Corps).

Stanhope. Captain, 4/4/1915.
5th April. Sun rises at 5.19 a.m. Sets 6.15 p.m. Moon rises at 1.18 p.m. Sets 7.57 a.m.

In the meantime, the 1st Canadian Division prepared their lines by digging deeper, piling sandbags and spreading barbed wire in front of their positions. A small rise, known as Gravenstafel Ridge, ran just behind the Canadian lines. Work was ordered to fortify this position, to prepare it as a secondary position should the frontline fall. In hindsight, the decision to entrench Gravenstafel Ridge would prove critical to the outcome of the impending battle.

On April 22, the Canadians held a three and one-half kilometre sector of the salient northwest of Ypres. To their left were troops from France's African colonies; to their right were British soldiers. At the junction of the French and Canadian lines was the 13th Battalion, Guy Drummond's unit. In addition to the 13th, there were three other Canadian battalions in the frontline. Four additional battalions were in direct support, just behind the front, camped near the village of St. Julien. Russ Boyle's 10th Battalion was being held in reserve with three other Canadian battalions at Ypres. As reserve units, these soldiers would only enter the battle if an emergency arose.

THE BATTLE BEGINS: THURSDAY, APRIL 22, 1915

April 22nd was a beautiful spring day. The men waited behind their defences and enjoyed the warm sun; a fresh, westerly breeze was blowing towards them. Reports indicated there was much activity behind the German lines. As the day unfolded, German shelling increased. Large shells began to explode in Ypres killing scores of inhabitants and many of the old brick houses were shattered by massive explosions. The famous Cloth Hall in the Market Square was set on fire. In their defensive positions, the men grew anxious, knowing an attack would soon follow.

At 5 p.m., the German shelling intensified and the bombardment became furious. The Germans opened the valves of the 5,500 gas cylinders that had been buried in their trenches and the westerly wind swept the gas forward. In front of the French Colonials, two large, curious yellow clouds rolled out of the German lines, joined up, and started floating towards them. There was an odd smell in the air and eyes suddenly became itchy. The gas attack had begun.

The Canadians adjacent to the French were not in immediate danger because the westerly wind was propelling the gas north of their positions and into the French lines. The huge cloud of gas, one kilometre thick and 700 metres wide, was moving at a speed of about eight kilometres an hour. As the Canadians watched the yellow gas billowing forward, they could see the French deserting their positions and running back towards Ypres. In their wake, they left a gaping hole about 12 kilometres wide on the left flank of the Canadians.

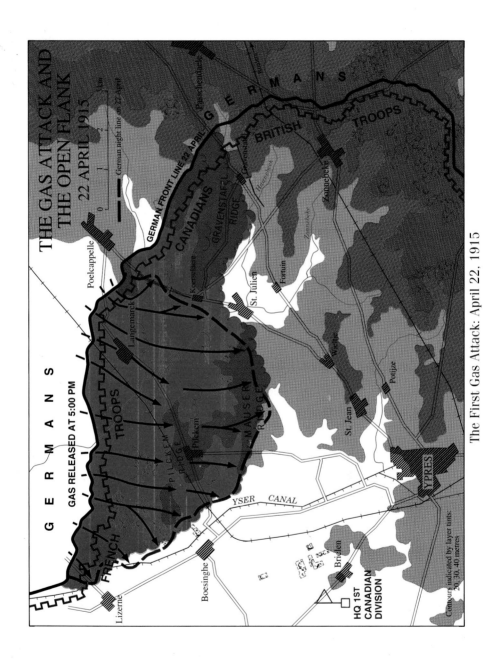

THE GAS ATTACK AND THE OPEN FLANK
22 APRIL 1915

The First Gas Attack: April 22, 1915

"...we noticed volumes of dense yellow smoke rising up and coming towards the trenches. We did not get the full effect of it...It makes the eyes smart and run. I became violently sick, but this passed off fairly soon. By this time the din was something awful - we were under a crossfire of rifles and shells, and had to lie flat in the trenches. The next thing I noticed was a herd of Turcos (French Colonial Troops) making for our trenches behind the firing line; some were armed, some unarmed. The poor devils were absolutely paralysed with fear."

J.D. Keddie, 15th Battalion.

The soldiers from Canada had no idea of what it was they were witnessing. But the sheer panic and desperate fear shown by the French soldiers was clear, even from kilometres away. Unanswered questions poured through their minds. Would they suffer the same fate as the French? What should be done about their wide-open flank? Would the Germans, attacking through the undefended gap, sweep behind their positions and surround them? One answer was certain; the Canadians would have to act decisively and quickly.

One hour after the gas attack began, the Canadians received their first orders to bring the chaos created by the fleeing French under control. At 6 p.m., units of the Canadian infantry were commanded to move into the open flank and, if possible, close it. At about the same time, the German infantry left their trenches. They had waited for the gas cloud to disperse into the atmosphere and it now seemed safe for them to attack. The Germans expected little resistance and believed that Ypres was there for the taking. But, they had not counted on the bravery and stubbornness of the 1st Canadian Division.

The first Canadian unit to engage the attacking Germans was the 13th Battalion from Montreal, the kilted, Royal Highlanders of Canada. Guy Drummond and his men quickly acted to stop the Germans. Moving into the empty French positions, they fired rapidly into the side of the German columns. At first, the Germans moved away from the devastating fire, but they were finally forced to confront the Montrealers. In a short, vicious fight, Drummond and his men were overwhelmed. Their sacrifice, however, was critical to the final outcome of the battle. By stopping the Germans from coming in behind the Canadian lines, they had prevented the 1st Canadian Division from being surrounded and they had deflected the main onslaught of the German attack northward.

A gun battery of the Canadian Field Artillery had noticed the desperate fighting between Guy Drummond's men and the attacking enemy.

To relieve the pressure on the Canadian defenders, the four guns of the artillery unit opened up on the German flank and inflicted many casualties. The harassing Canadian guns became an instant target for the approaching German infantry and a deadly race began between the artillerymen, who were trying to withdraw the precious guns, and the advancing enemy.

Sixty men led by machine-gunner Fred Fisher came to the assistance of the artillerymen. Fisher set-up his machine-gun in front of the Canadian guns and drove back several efforts by the Germans to capture them. The men with Fisher were all killed, but Fisher, in spite of the danger, continued to single-handedly shoot down the enemy until all the guns were safely away.

From Ypres and the ridges around it, the senior Canadian officers watched the battle unfold. They were terrified that the German attack through the gaping hole left by the French would wheel to the south, capture Ypres, and cut-off thousands of Canadian and British troops in the salient. There was no time to worry about the threat of another gas attack. The open flank would have to be closed.

Part of the Canadian troops held in reserve around Ypres were ordered forward to stop the German juggernaut and to close the open flank which was now seven kilometres wide. Time was in short supply. If the Germans acted quickly, they could surround the salient and trap the soldiers inside.

Almost immediately, the advancing reserve battalions confronted the enemy. North of the small village of St. Julien, men from Toronto, Montreal and Ottawa raked the German lines with heavy enfilade fire. In a series of small battles, they kept the Germans to the north of St. Julien and closed off a piece of the open flank, but they sustained heavy losses. As the battle raged, German artillery smashed the buildings in the threatened village and forced the Canadian defenders to dig for their lives.

By nightfall of the first day's fighting, the Germans had advanced and captured considerable territory, but St. Julien was still in Canadian hands and Ypres had not fallen. However, the enemy had occupied Kitchener's Wood, a heavily forested area just west of St. Julien. From this wood, the Germans could easily penetrate the Canadian positions, take the strategic village and march on to Ypres. Nightfall prevented further German attacks, but the morning could bring disaster. Kitchener's Wood would have to be taken.

"7a.m., April 22, 1915" by Arthur Nantel (CWM Cat.No.8629)

The Gas Attack At Ypres

The Canadians quickly realised that it was best to face the cloud, and hold on in the hope that the blindness would be temporary, and the cutting pain would pass away.

KITCHENER'S WOOD: MIDNIGHT, APRIL 22-23, 1915

The 1st Canadian Division still had four battalions held in reserve near Ypres. As the situation was desperate, the Generals decided two of the reserve battalions would capture Kitchener's Wood. The battalions ordered to make the attack were the 16th, a kilted battalion comprised of soldiers from British Columbia and Manitoba, and Russ Boyle's Albertans. These soldiers had no experience in battle, but none-the-less they were ordered to make a night attack against a position they had never seen. Even for the most experienced troops, a blind, night attack would be difficult, but asking 'green' troops to dislodge the Germans from Kitchener's Wood was almost asking the impossible. The fact that the Canadians did not know the exact location of the German forces within the Wood added further danger to the mission.

In the dark, 1,600 men marched two kilometres from Ypres towards St. Julien and arrived at their jump-off point just before midnight. Surrounded by the blackness of night, they formed up, as if on a parade square, and moved forward into the darkness, unsure of the exact location of Kitchener's Wood. In fact, the German positions in the Wood were only one and one-half kilometres to the north, but lay across open grain fields. Surprise was critical to the success of their attack and they moved quietly as they advanced. If the advancing Canadians were detected, the enemy would cut them done in swathes with machine-gun fire.

By some miracle, their approach went unnoticed until a number of men stumbled over a low, unseen hedge very close to the German lines. The ensuing noise alerted the enemy and the battle began.

"Then came the order to advance. Believe me there was some excitement in the ranks. We didn't seem to realize what we were up against. However we kept on going. When we got to 100 yards of the trench the "Huns" opened fire on us. The wood seemed to be literally lined with machine guns, and they played upon us with terrible effect. Our men were dropping thick and fast. However those remaining sailed right ahead and cleared the wood with a vengeance. A few Huns' were taken prisoners, but damned few."

J.C. Matheson, 10th (Alberta) Battalion.

"I vaguely saw some Germans, and rushed at the nearest one. My bayonet must have hit his equipment and glanced off, but luckily for me, another chap running beside me bayoneted him before he got me. By this

15

Battle of the Wood

The Tenth Battalion wins undying fame: the night attack on the wood near Saint-Julien, 22 April 1915.

time I was wildly excited and shouting and rushing into the wood up a path towards a big gun which was pointed away from us. Going through the wood we ran into several Germans, but I had now lost confidence in my bayonet and always fired."

An anonymous Canadian soldier, 16th(Canadian Scottish) Battalion.

The Canadians charged into Kitchener's Wood and the fighting became ferocious. Men fought with bayonets and rifle butts at close quarters in life or death combat. After three hours of terrible fighting, the Canadians had captured most of the Wood and had even managed to push out beyond it. However, pockets of German resistance remained and throughout the night sporadic rifle and machine-gun fire killed and maimed many of the Canadians who had survived the initial charge. Among the wounded was Russ Boyle, the Commander of the 10th Battalion. He had been cut down by a machine-gun strafe and had been shot five times in the groin. In great pain, he was taken from the battlefield for medical treatment.

Kitchener's Wood had been a costly battle with hundreds of men killed and wounded. The Canadian dead littered the battlefield and lay mixed with the corpses of the German dead. As the new day dawned, the survivors realized that the ground they had won at such great cost was too exposed to a massive German counter-attack. Reluctantly, the men slowly left the bloody scene and dug defensive positions just south of Kitchener's Wood. Later in the morning, they linked up with the Canadians at St. Julien. The attack on Kitchener's Wood had been poorly planned and bravely executed. The Canadian battalions had been bloodied badly in their baptism of fire, but their sacrifice had secured another piece of the open flank.

MAUSER RIDGE: FRIDAY, APRIL 23, 1915

For most of the Canadians, Friday, April 23 was a relatively quiet day. While German shelling of the Canadian lines was severe, they did not attack as expected. Surprisingly, many of the Canadian battalions were still in the same positions they occupied before the Germans had unleashed the poisonous gas the previous day. Soldiers from Winnipeg, Saskatchewan and Toronto still held their original lines and were yet to be attacked. Ominously, they waited behind their defences.

17

Their Commander, Arthur Currie, had watched the unfolding German attack closely. Although his men were not threatened at the moment, he knew their time would soon come. Currie wisely deducted the pivotal role that Gravenstafel Ridge would play in the forthcoming battle. Just behind his lines, a bump, known as 'Locality C' was the high point on Gravenstafel Ridge. Currie ordered Locality C transformed into a strong defensive position. In the days to come, it was to prove a fortunate decision.

Closer to Ypres, the open flank created by the fleeing French troops still had to be closed. The last two Canadian reserve battalions were instructed to attack a strong German position on Mauser Ridge, just south of the village of Pilkem. Mauser Ridge was typical of the insignificant rises in the topography of the salient. Almost imperceptible to the eye from a distance, control of these ridges gave the Germans the opportunity to rain murderous fire down on an attacking enemy. The Germans were keenly aware of their advantage on Mauser Ridge. They had worked feverishly throughout the night to entrench their position and by early Friday morning they had dug machine-gun emplacements and strung barbed-wire.

The order given to the 1st and 4th Battalions, men from Central and Western Ontario, to capture Mauser Ridge was similar to that given at Kitchener's Wood. The principal exception was the attack was to take place in daylight across open ground. The 1,600 men who were to secure Mauser Ridge could not have been happy with their order. They had been watching the Germans digging trenches and setting up their machine-guns.

To reach the German lines, the soldiers from Ontario would have to cross about half a kilometre of open farm field by first moving down a rise and then attacking up the other side directly into the enemy's field of fire. It was an almost impossible task.

At 5:25 a.m., the advance started. At first, the attack went well, but once they reached the depression at the foot of Mauser Ridge, the Germans opened up with machine-gun and rifle fire. Scrambling for their lives, and devoid of any cover, the Canadians had no choice but to entrench. At one point, they managed to capture a few farm buildings that offered some shelter from the murderous German fire, but they were driven out by artillery shelling that was often their own. The attack had failed. Trapped in the depression, little could be done to defend themselves but dig deeper and faster.

At 4:25 p.m., they tried again with the help of British reinforcements. But, it was not to be and the Germans retained command of the strategic ridge. In front of the German lines, the ground was littered with Canadian

Death of Colonel Birchall

"Its most gallant Commanding Officer, Lieut.-Colonel Birchall, carrying, after an old fashion, a light cane, coolly and cheerfully rallied his men, and at the very moment his example had infected them, fell dead at the head of the Battalion. With a hoarse cry of anger they sprang forward (for, indeed, they loved him) as if to avenge his death."

19

casualties. Of the 1,600 men who had attacked Mauser Ridge so bravely in the morning, more than 850 were dead, wounded or captured by the evening. Amongst the dead was the Commander of the 4th Battalion, Arthur Birchall, killed leading his men in the futile charge. Once again, inexperienced Canadian battalions had suffered terribly while undergoing their baptism of fire.

Surprisingly, by nightfall on April 23, the Germans had not made a major attack to further exploit their breakthrough and significant gains of the previous day. In fact, they were carefully massing their troops in anticipation of the morning of the 24th. This time the Canadians would meet the deadly gas head on.

THE GERMAN BREAKTHROUGH: SATURDAY, APRIL 24, 1915

By the third day of the battle, several Canadian battalions were still in their original trench lines and had not experienced a serious German attack. Among these units were kilted Montrealers and Torontonians of the 13th Battalion and 15th Battalion together with the 8th Battalion comprised of Winnipegers. These three battalions, totalling some 2,400 men, held an extremely vulnerable position known as the 'Apex'. The Apex was the point where the new left flank of the Canadian lines, established after two days of hard fighting, met the trench-lines of the Canadian soldiers who had yet to be attacked.

On a map, the Canadian lines at the Apex looked like a '7'. The position was very dangerous because it was exposed to attack from two directions. If the Germans broke through the Apex, they would be able to swoop down on the other Canadian battalions and encircle them. Anxiously, the men from Montreal, Toronto and Winnipeg strengthened their defences and awaited the inevitable attack.

As the men in the Apex waited, some good news about Germany's new secret weapon circulated through the trenches. Canadian Medical Officers had identified the gas the Germans had used as predominantly chlorine and developed a few defences against it. In the face of a chlorine gas attack, the men were advised to follow three defensive procedures. First, they were told to wet or urinate on a handkerchief or other cloth and hold it over their mouths and noses. Secondly, the Medical Officers, aware that chlorine gas is lighter than air and floats upwards, gave instructions for the men to hug the ground during a gas attack to reduce their exposure to the gas vapour.

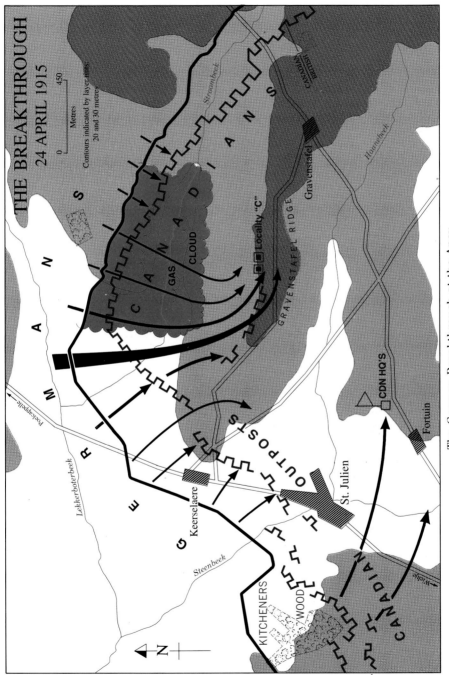

THE BREAKTHROUGH
24 APRIL 1915

Metres
0 — 450

Contours indicated by layer tints
20 and 30 metres

CANADIANS

CANADIAN
BRITISH

Stroombeek

Hannebeek

Locality "C"

GAS
CLOUD

GRAVENSTAFEL RIDGE

Gravenstafel

Poelcappelle

Lekkerboterbeek

CANADIANS

OUTPOSTS

CDN HQ'S

Fortuin

Keerselaere

St. Julien

Steenbeek

KITCHENERS

WOOD

CANADIAN

Wieltje

N

The German Breakthrough at the Apex

And thirdly, the men were ordered not to panic and run, but to stay still and allow the cloud of gas to pass over them, thus reducing the physical intake of gas. A fourth recommendation was just to hold their breath as long as possible!

At 4 a.m. on April 24, the expected German attack on the Apex began. A massive artillery barrage bombarded the Canadian front and a huge cloud of chlorine gas was released against the Torontonians of the 15th Battalion and the 8th Battalion from Winnipeg beside them. As they had been instructed, the men put wet or urine soaked cloths over their mouths and noses which gave them some protection, but the chlorine raked at their eyes and rendered them almost blind. Regardless of their precautions, the gas incapacitated the Canadians long enough for the German infantry, equipped with gas masks, to sweep across 'no man's land' behind the vapour cloud and reach the Canadian lines with minimal casualties.

"The greenish haze rose in front of the 3rd Brigade battalion and gradually extended to the right. It began to come over us like a fog bank...This wall of vapour, at least 15 feet in height advanced. The trench was a weird spectacle, men were spitting, cursing, grovelling trying to vomit...Men's bayonets looked as if they had been dipped in a solution of copper...the least exertion in the worst cases brought on choking, fit-like convulsions...as the fumes cleared away an attempt to attack our flank was met by so effective a machine-gun and rifle fire that 50 to 60 Germans were killed...the men wanted to kill and go on killing."

Anonymous Canadian officer, April 24, 1915.

The disabling effects of the chlorine gas and the sudden appearance of massed German infantry in front of their trenches proved a devastating combination for the hard pressed Canadians. Many were slaughtered where they stood, gasping for breath and unable to defend themselves. By 10 a.m., the Highlanders from Toronto were overwhelmed and routed, leaving a large gap in the centre of the Canadian lines. As the German infantry poured through, many of the Canadian positions along the Apex began to collapse. There was no choice but to retreat towards St. Julien. Even there, far from the original gas attack, the insidious chlorine vapour continued to plague the men, burning their throats and stinging their eyes.

"The effects of the successful gas-attack were horrible...All the dead lie on their backs, with clenched fists; the whole field is yellow...After fresh attacks a sleeping army lies in front of one of our brigades; they rest in

good order, man by man, and will never wake again - Canadian Divisions."
Rudolf Binding, German Army.

After breaking the Apex position, the advancing German infantry split and attacked in two directions. One group pursued the retreating Canadians as they fell back on St. Julien; the other German thrust wheeled around and slammed into the Canadian defences on the vital Gravenstafel Ridge.

There would be no sanctuary at St. Julien for the soldiers who were still reeling from the terrible effects of the poison gas. The German forces that were pursuing them quickly moved behind St. Julien. Simultaneously, another powerful German force pushed out from Mauser Ridge on the other side of the village and completed the encircling of the retreating Canadians. Over the next few hours, men from Ottawa, Montreal and Toronto, trapped in and around St. Julien, fought as small groups or even as individuals against the numerically superior enemy. Some escaped back to the Canadian lines, but by the end of the day, most were dead or had been captured.

While the battle for St. Julien raged, the Germans also pressed their assault against the Canadians defending Gravenstafel Ridge. The fate of the entire Canadian position in the Ypres salient now hinged on preventing the enemy from occupying this strategic position.

"Dawn saw the commencement of such a bombardment by the enemy as we had never in our wildest dreams imagined, and the powerful attacks that followed soon saw the Battalion... engaged in fighting for their lives, without knowledge of what was happening on their flanks. Murdered by that terrific fire, and driven back by sheer weight of numbers, they reformed and were driven back again, until nightfall found but a handful of men under a few officers, out of what had been a Battalion..."
History of the 7th (British Columbia) Battalion

"... half of the battalion had shot it out at close quarters - less than 100 yards - using rapid fire... they had done this from makeshift, incomplete emergency trenches, hastily dug the previous night in green fields dotted with acres of growing turnips. Where these grew right up to Canadian positions the turnip tops provided a screen for German infantry, who crawled into them from over a ridge... However the defenders had raked the turnips with a devastating fire... Thereafter they had crouched in a reserve trench, full of dead and dying..."
Harry Howland, 7th (British Columbia) Battalion

"The Second Battle of Ypres" by Richard Jack (CWM 8179)

The Canadians were determined to protect their lines and put up a heroic defence. At the foot of Gravenstafel Ridge, the 7th Battalion from British Columbia fought to the last bullet until they had to surrender. But their bravery bought valuable time for reinforcements to arrive. The next position attacked by the Germans was Locality C, the high point on the Ridge, which Currie had wisely fortified the previous day. The fighting for this important position was intense as men from several battalions attempted to repel the attackers. Even the capture of Locality C did not discourage the Canadians. They simply moved their defences to a farm 100 metres away. Finally, at this point, the line held and the Germans were denied complete control of Gravenstafel Ridge. Ypres was still safe.

Nightfall relieved the pressures of battle, but the day had gone poorly for Canada. Five Canadian battalions; one from British Columbia, two from Toronto and two from Montreal had been decimated and 1,400 men taken prisoner. The 15th Battalion had suffered 220 dead and 257 prisoners, the 7th Battalion lost 178 dead and 267 captured and the 13th Battalion, killed 124, captured 169. Roughly half of the soldiers in these battalions were killed or captured. Their sacrifice, however, had blunted the German onslaught and given time for the British to bring up reinforcements. The gas attack had been endured and valuable ground had been saved, but the Canadians had suffered terrible losses.

AFTER SHOCKS: SUNDAY, APRIL 25, 1915

Following the gas attack, and the loss of St. Julien and part of Gravenstafel Ridge, the exhausted Canadians were at their breaking point. Reinforcements were arriving, but another German assault could be too much for them to repel. The Germans, aware of the Canadian predicament, prepared to press their advantage.

Strangely, two Canadian battalions, the 8th from Winnipeg and the 5th from Saskatchewan, were still in the original positions they had held prior to the first gas attack. However, the German advance during the previous day had left them dangerously exposed. Roughly 1,000 Canadian soldiers were still out on the plain about one kilometre in front of Gravenstafel Ridge. The enemy was in front, beside and partially behind them.

As Sunday, April 25 unfolded, their position became even more precarious. The Germans, confident of their success, renewed their attack on the remaining positions on Gravenstafel Ridge, but were unable to push ahead much further. In a fighting retreat throughout the morning and

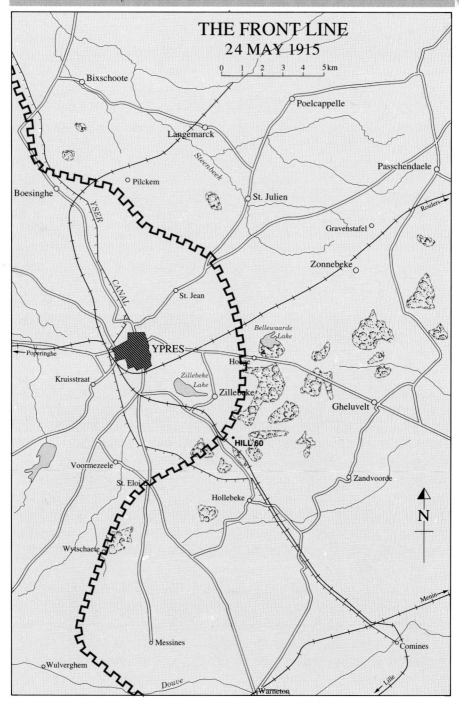

The Front Line: After the Battle

afternoon, the Canadians fell back on the little farms that dotted the Ridge and prevented any German breakthrough.

On the plain in front of Gravenstafel Ridge, the men from Winnipeg and Saskatchewan must have anxiously looked over their shoulders with every shot in anticipation of a German attack from behind. Finally, at mid-afternoon, they were ordered to withdraw to the Canadian positions on the Ridge. It must have been a great relief.

However, receiving orders to pull back was one thing; executing the orders successfully was another. As the Canadians were to discover, it is very difficult to disengage the enemy and retreat in the middle of a battle. When the withdrawal began at 6 p.m., the soldiers from Winnipeg and Saskatchewan were forced to cross a kilometre of open ground before reaching the safety of friendly trenches. German artillery mercilessly shelled the men as they withdrew and there were many casualties. It was not until the morning that the withdrawal was completed. Both battalions had managed the retreat very well and most of the men were saved from being trapped by the Germans. Still, the Canadians suffered many dead, wounded and men taken as prisoners of war.

After four days of heavy fighting, the 1st Canadian Division was finally taken out of the front lines. Depleted and exhausted, the men remained in the vicinity of Ypres for another week. Their fighting was over and their positions were taken over by fresh British troops, but they continued to suffer casualties from the incessant German shelling of the area. The remnants of the Canadian battalions were held in reserve at Ypres until early May when they were completely withdrawn from the salient. Not far from Ypres, each unit would refit, absorb new recruits to replace the many that were lost and prepare for the next battle. It was the first time that the Canadian battalions would undergo this process, but by the end of the war, most battalions would have 6,000 men pass through the ranks. In other words, over the duration of the war, each battalion would replace itself six times.

THE AFTERMATH

The Second Battle of Ypres continued until the end of May 1915. Gas was used again, but within a month it had lost its strategic value. Gas masks were already being issued to the troops. Never again would the use of gas present an opportunity like it did at Ypres. By the end of the battle, the British Army, including the Canadians, counted more than 59,000 dead, wounded or lost as prisoners of war. Of that number, 6,000 were Canadians, roughly half of all the Canadian infantrymen who saw action.

For Canada, it had been both a magnificent and tragic episode. Entering the front-lines prior to the battle, they had been 'Colonials', concerned whether they could uphold the honour of being 'British soldiers'. The Canadian troops, in their baptism of fire, had performed exceptionally. They had faced poison gas with no protection, fought against heavy odds and they had held. With firm determination, they had bought the time needed and they had saved a precarious situation. It was a remarkable beginning.

But this success could do little to console the families of 2,000 dead Canadian men. Their loved ones would see them no more, as if they had vanished into an unkind abyss. After the smoke of the battlefield cleared, there came the grim accounting that always follows modern battles. Who is dead, who is missing, who is wounded and who is a prisoner?

Gone was Russ Boyle, the rancher from Alberta, who died from wounds received at Kitchener's Wood. He left a widow and two children. Gone was Fred Fisher. His bravery in saving the guns won him a Victoria Cross. He was killed later in the battle and his body was never found. Guy Drummond was also missing. His mother, the influential Lady Drummond, was devastated, but less than two weeks later her daughter was drowned when a German U-boat sank the *S.S. Luisitania*. It is difficult to imagine her grief. In all, there were 2,000 stories like these. Husbands, brothers and sons who never returned.

In 1919, when the battlefields of Ypres were being cleared, the soldiers found a wooden cross with the inscription 'Unknown Canadian Officer - Royal Highlanders of Canada'. The makeshift grave was dug up and the remains of a very tall officer were found. By measuring the length of the femur, it was determined the officer had been 6' 3" in height. It was Guy Drummond. His remains were buried again in a Military Cemetery near St. Julien. The mystery surrounding his disappearance had been solved.

This was just the first time that Canada would undergo such massive grieving, but it was not to be the last. The telegrams would continue to be delivered and received in sorrow for three and one-half more years. Over 60,000 Canadians would die in the Great War. It was a high price to pay to bring the 'infant Dominion' a place in the World that was Canada's.

CANADA!
YPRES: APRIL 22-24. 1915.

SOME SLANG OF THE GREAT WAR

Alleyman - A German, from the French. Also Hun, Fritz, Boche, Jerry.

Batman - An Officer's servant, usually a Private.

Blighty - Refers to England. Also to a wound which would result in evacuation to a hospital in England.

Blind - Drunk. Also Blotto, Canned up, Muzzy, Zig Zag.

Blob - A glass of beer.

Bonce - The head.

Buchshee - Free or extra.

Butt-notcher - A sniper.

Canteen stinker - A poor quality cigarette. Cigarettes were also know as Fags, or Gaspers.

Chatt - A louse. Also to chatt was to sit amongst others and remove lice eggs from seams of clothing, etc. Also lousy.

Corpse ticket - Identity disks, worn around the neck. Two were worn, one was removed, the other was left with the body.

Crummy - Itchy due to lice bites. Also Hitchy-koo.

Dead soldier - Empty bottle of beer.

Dusty - All men named Miller, similarly Nobby Clark, Spud Murphy, Knocker White, Dan Coles, Timber Wood, Snowy Baker, etc.

Gone West - To be killed. Private Smith's gone west. Also to snuff it.

Hate - A bombardment. Usually in the morning or at set intervals during the day.

Jack Johnson - A large German shell, also called a coal-box. Named after the famous Heavyweight Champion.

Jake - Good. Also Jake-a-loo, Tray jake, etc.

Numbers up - Fatalistic feeling that his time was up and was about to be killed.

San Fairy Ann - It doesn't matter, makes no difference. Also Sweet Fanny Adams. From the French.

Third man on a light - A superstition that the third man to light a cigarette from the same match would sooner or later be killed. It was a very strong belief and soldiers would not allow anyone to be the third man. It was also practical as the light could be seen at night and therefore observed by snipers. The last words of H.H. Munro were "Put out that bloody cigarette."

Traverses - Thick partitions built into trenches to confine the effect of explosions and to prevent enfilading fire.

Wind-up - To be afraid. Also Windy.

TECHNOLOGICAL SLAUGHTER:
THE USE OF GAS AS A WEAPON

The Industrial Revolution of the 19th Century brought major developments in the world of Science and Engineering. Greater knowledge allowed the men of science to discover and exploit nature and the engineering field quickly developed the industrial processes to mass-produce many products. This technological progress marked an increase in the standard of living throughout the industrial world. The strength of science and technology, whether in industry or medicine, was making the World a better place.

But there was also a potential dark side to this era of progress. Those same scientists could easily turn their genius from helping people to killing people. It was the 'Great War' that first witnessed the advances of science being turned fully against mankind. More than any previous armed conflict, World War One would become a technological slaughter.

Throughout the war, the increased application of technology for military uses would result in important changes in the way battles were fought. Of all these technological developments, the most controversial was the use of gas as a weapon. Industrialization had enabled many types of gases to be mass-produced. In Europe, the concept of using gas in war had been contemplated prior to the end of the 19th Century. In fact, the issue had been discussed at an international conference at The Hague in 1899. It was decided that no civilized country would employ gas in war and a treaty was signed by the participants, including Germany, outlawing its use.

Prior to 1914, European wars had always been fought to a protocol whereby the belligerents adhered to a set of 'Gentlemen's' rules. Although violent, traditional warfare was also chivalrous and excesses that went beyond the norm were unacceptable. Most European wars involved a few battles after which the victor would claim some spoils, but the vanquished was always left with self-respect. The outbreak of the First World War changed this idealistic approach to warfare. From the outset, it was to be a fight to the finish. France would never cede an inch of its soil to Germany and only a total French defeat would satisfy the Germans.

More than any other event or technological development, the release of gas at Ypres marks the turning point that changed traditional warfare to total warfare. The 'Gentlemen's' wars were over; it was now the war of scientists. Once the decision was made to use gas, the development of the weapon was up to the scientists and the engineers. The generals and the politicians took a back seat as the men of science determined what gas to use and how to employ it in the most devastating manner.

First, the chemists had to decide on the properties of the gas that would be most effective. There were several types of gases that could prove useful as weapons. These included tear gas which affected the eyes, asphyxiators which incapacitated the lungs, toxins which attacked the central nervous system, sternutators which overwhelmed the respiratory system, and vesicants which blistered the skin.

Other properties also had to be considered. Importantly, the gas had to be difficult to defend against. An odourless gas, for instance, that lacked any pungent smell, would not forewarn the enemy. Likewise, an invisible gas could reach the enemy without prior detection. Two other characteristics were judged desirable. First, the gas could not be persistent. It had to be capable of dissipating quickly so that the attacking troops that had deployed the gas would not be harmed. And secondly, it could not be too reactive to air. If it were, atmospheric conditions could quickly neutralize its killing effect.

There was an even more important factor, however, which was the cost of production. Even war-mongers have budgets and whatever gas they selected had to be readily available and inexpensive. It was a cold-blooded decision.

Scientists from both sides worked on these problems throughout the war and evaluated more than 3,000 gases. In the end, only 12 met the requirements. At Ypres, the gas of choice was chlorine. It was readily available in Germany and it satisfied most of the properties required for an effective gas and a deadly weapon. The Germans first tried chlorine gas against the Russians with little effect. They had placed the gas in artillery shells, but its impact on the Russians was negligible. The skeptics of this new weapon must have been pleased. However, the scientists were given another chance. The location chosen for the next experiment was the Ypres salient in Flanders. This time the gas was compressed into cylinders which were put into the German front-line trenches. To be effective, the chlorine gas would have to be carried on a slight wind. At Ypres, they were confident of a westerly-wind that would carry the gas vapour towards the enemy trenches. The engineers had calculated that 152 tonnes of chlorine stored in 5,730 cylinders would be needed to give the desired impact.

At 5 p.m. on April 22, 1915, the valves of the cylinders were opened and within five minutes a billowing cloud of chlorine gas was approaching the French trench-lines. Overwhelmed, the desperate French deserted their positions and in their wake left a 12 kilometre gap in the front-line. The success of their secret weapon completely surprised the Germans. They had not assembled the necessary soldiers to fully exploit the breakthrough and the attack had been launched too late in the day for reserves to be brought forward. For the Canadians, who had to plug the breach in the line, the German miscalculation proved fortunate.

Chlorine gas was used again two days later against the Canadians with devastating results, but only a week after it was first deployed, counter-measures were already in place to nullify its effects. By the end of May 1915, gas masks were being issued to most British and French troops. Never again would gas create an opportunity like it did at Ypres in 1915.

"We went along the trench to where the smell was strongest. It was a most weird sight to see the men in their gas helmets made of flannel completely covering the head and tucking in under the collar, two eye holes covered with mica and a tube sticking out of their mouths to breath out of which closes automatically and cannot be breathed through. It is very comic to see two men trying to talk to each other. The flannel is quite thick and double in front of the mouth, there is a pad saturated with the dope... One man was staggering about the trench in a very gassed manner and I discovered that he had put on two helmets and was almost being suffocated."

Agar Adamson, Princess Patricia's Canadian Light Infantry

For the balance of the war, both sides continued to utilize various types of gas. The Germans tried a more toxic replacement for chlorine when they introduced phosgene in late 1915. Even though it was more deadly, it had a lesser strategic effect. Shortly after the first phosgene attack, the Allies modified their gas helmets to neutralize the new weapon. As the war progressed, other lethal gases were developed, but they were countered by other technical innovations.

In the later years of the war, gas was often employed against artillerymen to prevent the smooth operation of their heavy guns and to harass and affect the morale of soldiers in the front line. The gas was delivered in artillery shells or by projectiles fired from rudimentary mortars. Even if the gas were not a major weapon, it still terrified the soldiers in the trenches. The fear brought on by the ringing of the gas alarm is recounted in many memoirs of the First World War.

In 1917, the Germans, realizing that their use of lethal gases was not achieving the expected battlefield results, made an strategic decision.

DULCE ET DECORUM EST

Bent double, like old beggars under sacks,
Knock-kneed, coughing like hags, we cursed through sludge,
Till on the haunting flares we turned our backs,
And towards our distant rest began to trudge.
Men marched asleep. Many had lost their boots,
But limped on , blood-shod.
All went lame; all blind;
Drunk with fatigue; deaf even to the hoots
Of gas-shells dropping softly behind.

Gas! Gas! Quick, boys! - An ecstasy of fumbling,
Fitting the clumsy helmets just in time;
But someone still was yelling out and stumbling
And floundering like a man in fire or lime
Dim, through the misty panes and thick green light,
As under a green sea, I saw him drowning.

In all my dreams, before my helpless sight,
He plunges at me, guttering, choking, drowning.
If in some smothering dreams, you too could pace
Behind the wagon that we flung him in,
And watch the white eyes writhing in his face,
His hanging face, like a devil's sick of sin;
If you could hear, at every jolt, the blood
Come gargling from the froth-corrupted lungs,
Obscene as cancer, bitter as the cud
Of vile, incurable sores on innocent tongues
My friend, you would not tell with such high zest
To children ardent for some desperate glory,
The old Lie: Dulce et decorum est Pro patria mori.

Wilfred Owen (1893-1918)

Moving away from asphyxiants, they developed an effective vesicant, the infamous mustard gas. The introduction of mustard gas marked a new stage in the development of gas warfare. Unlike the previous gases, which had been designed to damage the respiratory system, mustard gas attacked the surface of the body. It severely blistered the skin and could also cause blindness. Consequently, gas masks offered little defence against this new threat. Mustard gas was also persistent. It hung in the air until it was absorbed by the earth or clothing. As a result, it could cause casualties months after it was deployed. To make matters worse, the almost odourless mustard gas often caught the soldiers unprepared.

The first use of mustard gas was near Ypres in July 1917, when the gas was deployed in artillery shells. One million shells were fired into the British positions resulting in more than 15,000 casualties. The strategy involved with the use of mustard gas was not to kill, but to injure or harass. The Germans knew a wounded man was more expensive in terms of resources than a dead one. Although mustard gas was never really countered, the war became mobile in early 1918 and greatly reduced the opportunities for its use. Its legacy of attacking the economics and logistics of war was a devastatingly 'cold' concept for waging war. So, in the end, was the use of mustard gas a more humane type of war?

The fear of gas was apparent in the precautions taken by British civilians during 'The Blitz' in the early stages of the Second World War. They were issued with gas masks, but their precautions were not necessary and gas played no role as an offensive weapon during the Second World War. Had mankind learned its lesson?

No. Today the offspring of that infamous day at Ypres threaten the World. Technological slaughter is easier now than ever. Science has made major advancements since 1915 and with its humanitarian developments, came the black, evil side of science, with its objective the destruction of man. The scientists can now produce more insidious and lethal products than their predecessors ever dreamed of. Nerve gases and biological products now available to so many countries can reap a harvest of death that makes the chlorine gas attack at Ypres in 1915 look civilized.

"IN FLANDERS FIELDS"

The classic poem of The Great War, "In Flanders Fields", was written by a Canadian Army Medical Corps officer in May 1915. John McCrae penned the verse near Essex Farm, along the Canal de l'Yser north of Ypres after a week of shocking action. Although a veteran of the Boer War, McCrae would have seen nothing like the suffering that went on at the Second Battle of Ypres. On the morning of May 2, a German heavy shell burst in the Canadian artillery positions on the banks of the Canal de l'Yser, killing instantly McCrae's good friend Lieutenant Alexis Helmer of Ottawa. Lieutenant Owen Hague of Montreal was mortally wounded by the same shell. Helmer's death had a profound affect on McCrae, who was moved to write "In Flanders Fields" the following day. The poem was published in *Punch* Magazine in December 1915. McCrae died of pneumonia at Wimereux, France, January 28, 1918 at the age of 45.

IN FLANDERS FIELDS

In Flanders Fields the poppies blow
Between the crosses, row on row,
That mark our place; and in the sky
The larks, still bravely singing, fly
Scarce heard against the guns below.

We are the dead. Short days ago
We lived, felt dawn, saw sunset glow,
Loved, and were loved, and now we lie
In Flanders Fields.

Take up your quarrel with the foe:
To you from failing hands we throw
The torch; be yours to hold it high.
If ye break faith with us who die
We shall not sleep, though poppies grow
In Flanders Fields.

THE NATIONALITIES WHO SERVED

Immigration to Canada between 1880 and 1914 swelled Canada's population; the 1911 census counted 7.2 million Canadians, a 50% increase since 1880. The magnet of free land in Western Canada attracted new immigrants in droves, not only from the British Isles, but also from Russia, Scandinavia, Japan, the United States and a host of other countries.

Sixty-four percent of the original Canadian contingent that sailed for Europe in the autumn of 1914 was British-born, but by the end of the war, Canadian-born soldiers made up 52% of total enlistment. However, the statistics, which are based on the country of birth, do not reflect the fact that many of the men who were listed as British-born were actually raised in Canada.

Also, the different attitude towards the definition of British citizenship in those days must be examined. For a British citizen, emigrating to one of the dominions or colonies was not considered to be entering a foreign country. Canada was further than moving to Devonshire, but it was still part of the Empire.

As a result, the high percentage of British-born soldiers in the 1st Canadian Division is not surprising. What is surprising is the extent of the many different nationalities that enlisted. Throughout the war, 12% of all enlistment came from men who were not born in Canada or the British Isles. These soldiers were born in such diverse countries as Italy, Switzerland, Belgium, France, Norway, Sweden, Denmark, Iceland, Greece, Montenegro, Egypt, Russia, Venezuela, Argentina, Mexico, and the United States, to name just a few.

	The 1st Canadian Contingent Enlistments	Total Enlistments in the Canadian Expeditionary Force
	1914	1914-1919
CANADA	10,880 (30%)	318,705 (52%)
BRITISH ISLES	23,211 (64%)	228,174 (36%)
OTHER COUNTRIES	176 (6%)	72,757 (12%)

The above table clearly illustrates the enthusiasm of recent British immigrants to defend the Empire. Of interest is the fact that the second contingent to sail for Europe was predominantly British-born as well. The statistics pertaining to those born in Great Britain reveal the following breakdown: 69% English; 21% Scottish; 8% Irish; and 2% Welsh. The keenness of those who had immigrated to Canada from other Empire countries was also to be expected. For the most part, they were white colonials from New Zealand, Australia, South Africa, Ceylon, India, Newfoundland and the British West Indies.

The table also chronicles the increasing enthusiasm of men born in other countries to enlist as the war progressed. These men were principally Americans who had either immigrated to Canada or who had crossed the border to participate in the great adventure. Still, the wide dispersion of nationalities that fought for Canada is fascinating.

The white man's 'Great War' also attracted others in Canada to join the colours: the Japanese-Canadians; the Sikhs; Black Canadians; and Native Canadians. Though they were considered, by the men who ran the war, to be lesser races and ignorant children, in that non-malicious 'that is all you can expect of them' racism of the period, they still enlisted and served with pride. German names do crop up on the enlistment documents, but many German Canadians were interned during the war.

BIBLIOGRAPHY - SUGGESTED READING

Welcome to Flanders Fields by D.Dancocks: McClelland and Stewart, 1988.

Beyond Courage by G. Cassar: Oberon Press, 1985.

Letters of Agar Adamson edited by N.M.Christie: CEF BOOKS, 1997.

The Official History of the Canadian Expeditionary Force, 1914-1919 by G.W.L. Nicholson: The Queen's Printer, 1962.

The Canadians at Ypres, April 22nd-26th 1915 by Norm Christie: CEF BOOKS, 1996.